308

Minibeasts
Questions and Answers

Written by Gerald Legg
Edited by Philippa Moyle

Contents

Many young minibeasts look like small versions of their parents. They simply grow into adults. Others look completely different. They develop into adults through stages.

Some young minibeasts that look like small adults, such as snails, grow very gradually. Others, such as insects, have a hard outer skeleton. They have to moult in order to grow.

They moult by making a new, soft skeleton beneath the hard one. The new skeleton is pumped up with air, and this splits the old skeleton. The young minibeast grows inside the new, hard skeleton.

A Young **scorpions** are carried on their mother's back while they grow.

A

Cockroaches lay their eggs in a hard purse-shaped case. When the young hatch, they look like small adults.

Cockroaches can produce 30,000 young in a single year!

A

Young **snails** look like miniature adults when they hatch from round, silvery-coloured eggs. As they grow, more coils are added to their shells.

grow?

A Young **damselflies** are called nymphs. The nymphs crawl up plant stems out of the water. The young adults pull themselves out of their nymphal skins.

Smaller banded snail

A Young **spiders** are often carried about by their mother.

Earthworms keep their tails in their burrows when they mate, so they can escape if there is danger.

Snails and earthworms are hermaphrodites. This means that they make both eggs and sperm. When they mate, they exchange sperm and fertilize each other's eggs.

When they are born, many young minibeasts look completely different from their parents. They go through several stages to develop into adults.

The young that hatch from the eggs are called larvae. A larva feeds and grows. It eventually develops into a chrysalis, which is also called a pupa. Inside the chrysalis, the larva changes into an adult. After a time, the adult emerges from the chrysalis.

The development of a larva into an adult through these stages is called metamorphosis.

A **Ladybird beetles** and their larvae feed on aphids.

A

A **caddis fly larva** develops into a chrysalis in its home. It then leaves its home and swims to the water surface to become an adult.

A

The larvae of **butterflies** and **moths** develop into adults through metamorphosis.

This egg has been laid by a **pasha** butterfly.

This **pasha** caterpillar will turn into a chrysalis.

Caddis fly larvae live underwater. They make homes to live in by sticking together pieces of plant, sand, shells and other material. They carry their homes around with them.

You can watch young caterpillars grow by keeping them in a jar with some;food. You should ask an adult to make a hole in the lid of the jar. Cover the jar with greaseproof paper with tiny holes in it, and replace the lid. This will allow the caterpillars to breathe.

A **Black fly larvae** live in streams and ponds. They attach themselves to rocks with the sucker on their rear.

Adult black flies suck blood. Some of them carry diseases which they inject when they suck the blood.

Inside the chrysalis, the **pasha** caterpillar changes.

The adult **pasha** butterfly emerges from the chrysalis.

Minibeasts have to find food to eat in order to grow. Some of them eat the leaves, shoots, flowers, fruits and roots of plants. Many minibeasts even eat other minibeasts!

Minibeasts find their food in different ways. Some of them eat rotten plants or animals, while others suck juices from plants, or even blood from animals!

Some minibeasts tunnel and burrow through the soil, while others hunt for a meal on the surface of the ground. Some minibeasts even make traps in which they catch their prey.

A

Net-throwing spiders spin a net and throw it over their prey as it walks underneath.

Animals that hunt other animals are called **predators**.

Animals that are hunted are called **prey**.

Animals that eat other animals are called **carnivores**. Animals that eat plants are called **herbivores**.

A

Long-jawed spiders are well camouflaged on grass as they wait to trap their prey as it walks past.

A

Trap-door spiders hide in a silk-lined burrow with a trap door at the entrance. They throw open the trap door to grasp their prey.

hunt?

A **Praying mantids** are very well camouflaged. They seize their prey with their spiney forelegs and feed on it upside-down.

A

Antlion larvae lie half-hidden at the bottom of a funnel-shaped pit. They flick sand at minibeasts that slip over the edge of the pit, so that the minibeasts fall down to the bottom.

A **Blue-black spider wasps** have a loud buzz which terrifies their prey.

Euglandina rosea attacking a *papustyla* snail.

A

Tiger beetles are fierce hunters. They use their strong jaws to kill and cut up their prey, which includes young lizards.

A **Snails** sometimes attack and eat other snails. If the snail has withdrawn inside its shell, the attacker will drill a hole through the shell to eat the snail.

Some minibeasts live on liquid food. They have extremely sharp mouthparts which they use to pierce the skin of an animal or the tissue of a plant.

They usually suck blood or plant juices through a sucking tube.

A

Oleander Hawkmoths hover in the air like hummingbirds. Their tongues are 12 cm long. They use them to suck nectar from deep within a flower.

A

Fleas use the hooks and spines on their bodies to hold tightly on to the fur or skin of their hosts. Fleas can carry diseases which they inject into their hosts when they bite.

In the Middle Ages, the disease called the Black Death was spread by the rat flea. This disease killed millions of people.

A

Ticks are parasites. They sink their hooked mouthparts into the flesh of their host. As they suck the blood, their round, elastic bodies swell greatly.

A **Aphids** feed on plant juices. Their delicate mouthparts pierce the sap vessels inside a plant, and the pressure forces sweet-tasting sap into the aphid's body.

Some of the sap is passed out of the aphid as a drop of sweet fluid. This is sometimes eaten by ants.

feed?

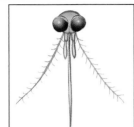

The long, needle-sharp mouthparts of a mosquito contain a sucking tube.

A **Mosquitoes** feed on blood and plant juices. Female mosquitoes have a meal of blood before they lay their eggs. Male mosquitoes suck plant juices instead of blood.

Female mosquitoes bite humans. A person can lose over half a litre of blood in an hour.

A **Jungle leeches** suck blood. When they have had a meal, their body swells.

Animals that live and feed on other animals are called **parasites**. The animals that provide a home and food are called **hosts**.

A **Thrips** are tiny 'thunder-bugs'. They have mouthparts on one side of their mouth only, which they use to suck plant juices.

Thrips are pests, feeding on corn and other crops.

A **Robber flies** catch and stab their prey with their sharp mouthparts. Their victim is then sucked dry.

A **Cochineal bugs** suck plant juices. They are used to make food colouring as they are dark red.

Minibeasts have to get about in order to find food, a mate and a new place to live. They also need to be able to escape from predators.

Minibeasts use many ways of getting about. Some of them crawl and others run. Some of them jump and others wriggle. Some of them can even fly.

Most minibeasts that fly have two pairs of wings which beat together.

A Spiders can fly but do not have wings! This **Wolf spider** has released a long, silken thread. The wind will pluck the thread into the air, whisking the spider away.

A **Beetles** have two pairs of wings. The first pair is very tough and protects the delicate flying wings which are folded underneath when not in use.

A

Dragonflies chase other flying minibeasts by rapidly beating their outstretched wings.

Emperor dragonfly

A

Damselflies fly by fluttering their wings. They catch other flying minibeasts by grasping them with their legs.

A **Butterflies** fly during the daytime. Most of them slowly flap their large, colourful wings.

Flies are brilliant acrobats. They can even land upside down.

The wings of the **painted lady** warn other minibeasts to keep away.

A

Flies have only one pair of real wings. The rear wings are tiny bat-shaped objects which beat very fast.

The wings of the **swallowtail** make a noise as they clap together.

A **Hover flies** can hover, dart backwards and forwards, and even fly straight upwards.

A **Midges** have one of the fastest wing beats. Some beat their wings over 1000 times a second.

A **Fairy flies** have delicate, feathery wings. They are one of the smallest flying minibeasts.

A **May bugs** fly at dusk. They can fly over five kilometres in search of a mate.

Q How do minibeast

Many minibeasts get about by crawling or running. Some of them have lots of short legs which they use to crawl about.

Other minibeasts have fewer legs, but they are usually quite long. Long legs allow the minibeast to run about quickly.

A **Pseudoscorpions** can run backwards as well as forwards! They are active hunters that crawl amongst decaying leaves in search of a meal.

Pseudoscorpions have long sensitive hairs on their rear to help them feel where they are going.

A

Caterpillars have special suckers, called prolegs, on their bodies which keep them firmly fixed on to twigs and leaves, even in a strong wind.

A

Common house centipedes have 30 legs. Some of the legs are longer than others so that they do not trip themselves up!

A

Harvest spiders have very long leg and a small body. To prevent then from toppling over, they bend their legs and keep their body close to the ground.

The legs of harvest spiders are not used for speed. The spiders crawl through the vegetation where they live.

12

Caterpillars usually have plenty of food around them. As they do not need to move far to find a meal, they have short legs.

A **Millipedes** have over 100 pairs of legs which they use to crawl along the ground.

Privet hawkmoth caterpillar

A **Jewel beetles** scurry about in search of food. They have beautiful coloured wing cases. In South America, they are used as living jewellery which is why they are called jewel beetles.

A **Huntsman spiders** hide underneath the bark of a tree while they wait for their prey. They then race to catch it using their long legs.

Golden huntsman spider

A **Woodlouse-eating spiders** have enormous jaws which are specially designed to catch woodlice

All spiders have eight legs, which they use to run about.

Some minibeasts move about by hopping and jumping. Being able to jump suddenly is a good way to catch a meal, or to escape from a predator.

Other minibeasts skate across the surface of water in search of food or a mate.

A **Raft spiders** stand half on the water and half on a water plant. They race across the water surface to catch their prey, which includes small fish.

A **Grasshoppers** and **crickets** use their strong back legs to catapult themselves high into the air.

A **Fleas** have large back legs which allow them to jump very high - well over half a metre.

Fleas jump on to animals, such as cats, where they make their home.

A **Treehoppers** hop from tree to tree in search of food.

A **Pond skaters** have waterproof hairs on their feet which help them to float on the water surface.

hop, jump and skate?

Grasshoppers attract a mate by rubbing their back legs against their front wings to make a singing sound.

A **Springtails** can spring suddenly into the air using their special 'tail'.

The 'tail' is tucked under the springtail's body.

The 'tail' straightens suddenly, making the springtail spring into the air.

A

Jumping plant lice have very strong back legs which means they can jump from plant to plant.

Apple suckers are jumping plant lice which live on apple trees.

A **Click beetles** have a peg on their bodies. When they lie on their backs and bend, the peg pops free with a loud click, and they jump into the air.

A

Whirligig beetles skate quickly across the surface of a pond in a zigzag pattern.

A

Jumping spiders have excellent sight. When they see a fly, they will leap into the air to catch it.

Legs can get in the way, so some minibeasts do not have any legs at all. They have soft bodies, and they move about by slithering along the ground or wriggling through the soil.

Earthworms make burrows which let air into the soil. They drag leaves into the burrows for food.

 A

Leeches move along by using their suckers. They have two suckers on their bodies, one at the front and one at the rear. The one at the front has teeth as it is also their mouth.

The rear sucker sticks to the ground and the body stretches forward.

The front sucker sticks to the ground and the body is pulled forward.

African giant snail

You can make a wormery by putting some earthworms and compost into a plastic bucket with small holes in the bottom. As the earthworms eat the compost, you will need to add some more to the bucket.

A

Earthworms burrow through the soil by eating it. They grip the soil with very small bristles along their bodies.

slither and wriggle?

A

Slugs and snails are special minibeasts that slither along on a trail of slime using one foot. If you place a slug or snail on a piece of clear plastic and look at it from underneath, you will see ripples moving along the foot as the minibeast moves forward.

A

Hover fly larvae look like little leeches. They wriggle along in search of aphids which they eat.

A

Fly larvae hatch from eggs laid on dung. They have small legs, or no legs at all. To move about, they wriggle through their squidgy food.

A

Soil centipedes have up to 100 pairs of tiny legs which help them to grip the soil.

A

Nematodes are minute roundworms which live inside many animals and plants, and in soil. They move about by wriggling their tiny bodies.

17

Some minibeasts hide from predators or prey, while others display bright colours, make noises, or glow at night to attract attention.

Many minibeasts use colours and shapes to disguise themselves. Some blend into their background, which is called camouflage. Others pretend to be fierce minibeasts.

Some minibeasts use bright colours to frighten or warn their predators. Others use sound and light to 'talk' to each other and attract a mate.

A **Assassin bug larvae** look like the surrounding soil.

A **Peppered moths** blend into the bark of the tree trunk on which they are resting.

Some Peppered moths are darker. They hide on tree trunks which have been blackened by pollution.

A **African bush-crickets** are perfectly camouflaged among the leaves.

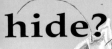
hide?

 Stick insects are well hidden from predators as they look like the twigs they are sitting on.

Stick insects can be kept in a large jar as pets.

 **Banded snails** have different shells.

The snails with pale shells live in dry, pale green grass.

The snails with dark shells live in lush green vegetation.

 Flower mantids are well camouflaged as they lie in wait for their prey.

Brimstone butterflies look like the green ivy leaves that they rest on.

 **Crab spiders** are predators that hide within flowers, waiting to pounce on visiting insects.

Many minibeasts use bright colours to protect themselves. Some of them frighten their predators by suddenly flashing bright colours at them.

Some minibeasts show their bright colours all the time. Predators learn that these are warning colours, telling them that the minibeast is dangerous.

There are only a few warning colours: black, white, yellow, red and brown. Minibeasts learn quickly that these colours warn of danger.

A **Peacock butterflies** have large colourful eye spots on their wings.

A **Puss moth caterpillars** shoot out long red tassles from tubes on their rear when they are frightened.

warn?

A **South African grasshoppers** have brightly coloured bodies which warn other minibeasts to keep away.

A **Owl butterflies** become fierce creatures with large, staring eyes when their wings are spread open.

Owl butterflies look like leaves with their wings folded.

A **Cotton stainer bugs** are left alone by birds because of their warning colours.

A **Praying mantids** rise up and startle their predators with a brilliant pattern of colours.

A **Lantern bugs** have colourful wings. They warn predators to keep away.

Many minibeasts use sound to attract a mate, or to warn off predators. Some of them make sounds during the day. If you walk through a field or a forest, you may hear all kinds of chirps and buzzes.

Many minibeasts make sounds at night, while others use light to attract a mate. The males or females glow in the dark, and their mates are attracted to them.

A Katydids sing their repetitive song 'katydid, katydidn't' at night. They sing by rubbing their left front wing against a ridge on the right wing.

Katydids and other crickets have ears on their legs.

A Tree crickets make thousands of piercing chirps without stopping. Some tree crickets can be heard 1.6 km away!

sing and glow?

A Silkmoths fly at night. They squeak when they hear the sounds made by bats. The squeaks confuse the bats which leave the silkmoths alone.

A Fireflies flash across the night sky to attract a mate.

A Queen honeybees squeak by squeezing air through tiny holes in their bodies.

A Glow-worms are beetles that glow at night.

A Death watch beetles bang their heads against the sides of their burrows!

Index

Gerald Legg PhD FRES FZS is Keeper of Biology at the Booth Museum of Natural History, Brighton, England, where he regularly answers children's questions on minibeasts. He has also worked and lived in Africa, studying minibeasts in the rainforest.

This edition specially produced for School Book Fairs by Zigzag Publishing Ltd, 5 High Street, Cuckfield, Sussex RH17 5EN

Series concept: Tony Potter
Senior Editor: Nicola Wright
Design Manager: Kate Buxton
Designed by: Nicky Linzey, Anne Wright, Chris Leishman
Illustrated by: Maggie Brand, Peter Bull, Wayne Ford/Wildlife Art Agency, Jackie Harland, Bridgette James/Wildlife Art Agency, Ruth Lindsey, Steven Young

Colour separations: ScanTrans, Singapore
Printed in Italy

First published 1993
10 9 8 7 6 5 4 3 2 1

Original material copyright © 1993 Zigzag Publishing Ltd. This edition copyright © 1993 Zigzag Publishing Ltd.

ISBN 1874647 18 6